CRACKED CALABASH

Other titles from Central Square Press

A HARD SUMMATION by Afaa Michael Weaver

CRACKED CALABASH

poems

Lisa Pegram

CENTRAL SQUARE PRESS

All inquiries and permissions requests should be addressed to the Publisher:
Central Square Press
P.O. Box 2621
Lynn, MA 01903

publisher@centralsquarepress.com
www.centralsquarepress.com

Published in the United States of America
First Edition

ISBN-13: 978-1-941604-01-4

ISBN-10: 1941604013

Thank you to the editors of the following publications in which these poems first appeared:

The Academy of American Poets (poets.org): "After Dinner"; Songs of Root & Branch: "Latte," "Snorkeling," "Lighthouse" (musical score; David Arbury, composer)

Cover art: "19th Century Hawaiian Calabash Medicine Bowl"

For my beloved grandmother & lighthouse,
Dr. Margaret G. Dabney

CONTENTS

INTRODUCTION

CRACKED CALABASH, being a collection that contemplates personal identity in the context of healing and self-love, is more process than destination, and rightfully so. This vessel of thirteen poems provides an opportunity to sit in on a conversation about joy and suffering, love and belonging, and the reconciliation of self in the midst of a painful search for truth.

It does not take much time to discover that this collection is crafted by a poet whose pen has cracked open a portal. Cracked, as in a gateway, an opening. Cracked, as in left ajar. As in a cracked door or cracked skin, cracked shell. These poems open and shut rooms, and are unhindered in their delicate interrogation and suture of wounds.

Lisa Pegram, in her debut chapbook of poetry, brings forth a fierce set of poems that are rooted in the notion that *there is wisdom and even joy to be found in the places where we are broken and put back together again.*

—*Enzo Silon Surin*, Publisher

cracked calabash

Lime Pickle

after Kathy Sosa

In this memory

I carry a basket full of ripe avocados. Sliced open,
their pits are exposed, an armful of eyes cradled
between my hips. They are soft, green

and stare without blinking.

My shoulder is the color of the caramelo
that sits on top of flan. I never noticed
then, how warm and sweet my brown was,

with all the fuss about keeping it covered.

I trade skin for cloth. Linen stained turquoise,
tangerine or marigold. Washed soft by hand,
faded by sun. Fastened with sea glass or bottle caps.

I refuse to wear a slip, I am young old, a Doña
newly hatched. Not yet comfortable with my hair
pinned up, knees covered, shades drawn.

Where is the night owl that used to perch in my ribs and sing?

The avocados are for my Persian neighbor,
who teaches me to cook saffron rice with a crust of potato
on the bottom of the pot. To fatten the grains by spooning
yogurt into the rice water.

To dry bowls of whole limes in the back porch sun.

We pickle huge mason jars of garlic, eggplant and baby carrots,
to be soaked soft by months in vinegar. I marvel at how quiet
and small she becomes in the kitchen, tucked tight

inside her mother-in-law's recipes. She is bite sized. She is
every slice of onion,

which no longer make her eyes water. I ask about her
mother's best dishes
or perhaps, her own. She drains the rice. Chops mint,
cucumber and tomato
for salad. Says nothing. The twitch above her eye reminds me

to wash a load of laundry when I get home. And water
the plants.

Last Rite

I. Wring
I am only a child.

II. Choke
a lap full of salt water
a dried calabash bulleted with holes
turned sieve

moonlight poured into an open mouth.

III. Confess
a nightmare with hooves
and a saddle
tiny girls bathe in a dirty well

a chapped hand over a pink mouth.

IV. Twist
woolen hair woven into silk
a carpet full of dust
bare feet on broken glass

a wooden spoon banging on a pot, bowing across a rake.

V. Blink
a bed split in three
a rusted knife between legs
that run in mid air

a goat roasting outside a hut.

VI. Break
Today, you be woman.

Uplift the Race, 1928

Darling, We have passports

and We use them. If you want to get out
of the box, you must travel in the right
circles. Think W.E.B. , not Booker T,
n'est ce pas? Summer at Idlewild or the Inkwell
Ah! The Vineyard. Cotillions and cocktails—Try

to be as 'Not Black' as possible, all the while choosing
to remain Black, you see? No flies in the buttermilk.
Black skin cleaves to the field. Sun's lash. Illiterate
funk. Dine from the trough? No, be White-Black (Fork
on the left, knife on the right.) There is a difference.

Bind your swarthy parts tight to your chest
with stretched cotton. Everyone who's anyone
knows the flat front is all the rage—ropes
of long pearls lie unmolested against it.

This does not mean deny your race. Heavens,
on the contrary. We re-define The Race. Curse
the banjo and slave narrative, We create
improvisational jazz and surrealist art. We write
poetry and read Proust. Go to the symphony

and enjoy it. Tucked neatly beneath the radar, We
are a most moveable feast (though plagued
with a curious, chronic indigestion.)

Disowned

Baby sister, so pale you were green
in the cradle, wicked little cry sweeping
a metal rake across a wooden floor.

Anna means "Favour." You, tiny fist
raised, ruled a house of monkeys bowing
so low to something so tiny. Mama

let you sleep in the front room with her.
Bassinet grew into a bed. Daddy ticked
away his sentence on the guest room wall.

Laius had the right idea. This gift, end
of our joy. How milk soured at touch
of your mouth. Curdled

in your Buddha belly, a constant bile brewing.
Had we known, we would have pushed you
harder on the swing. Higher, so wind lifted

you off your seat. Grip yanked from chain,
legs still pumping, your protest

an emerald balloon in a white sky.

Latte

Grind the crime—strong and dark
into obedient powder. Spoon

into filter. Press. Fill
the mouth with boiling water

until all that's left is confession.
(Inadmissible.) Pour

into ceramic cup. Set
aside. Steam milk

gently. Take care, decrease
heat before foam

begins to rise. Drown
blackness until all that's left

is fleeting shadow. *Father forgive
me.* Add sugar to taste. Or not.

While cooling say ten Hail
Mary's. Sip

slowly. Relish
bitterness at the bottom.

Lighthouse

Hushed black child in the attic practices art of the flash.
Mirror angled in the sun, beams warn by the flash.

Day-marked body, narrow spiral of white   black
imitates disbelief—a blink—sight torn by the flash.

Fair skin with cruel tongues, waves crest and fall.
Albatross pierced by lightning, adorned by the flash.

Cursed depths. Face down. Stark surface roar.
Dark meat. Shark pattern. Souls mourned by the flash.

Clock in the chest, wick in the mind, acetylene courses
her veins. *One day   my womb   shall transform by the flash.*

Candle on the Water, melody in reverse, haunting
the past. Pluck the strings. Tap the drum. Blow the horn by the flash.

This Pharos is more Moses, warm beacon slicing cold sea.
Consecrated to God—marked by flesh but firstborn of the flash.

Snorkeling

Around you.

Everywhere

all the time

Tiny currents, tiny pulls
en masse. Touching you and not. Flashing
light, not haunting but en route.   *Could spirits
be like this?*   Bursts   you can't see,

all those fish.

Swimming

Before, when you've been in the sea,
did you realize? All those times,
salt crystal baking in the sun.

they tessalate   *whisper*

across skin. More color combinations
than one imagination can hold.

Turquoise   tangerine

lungs collapse into schools of magenta. Your eyes
opened, the first time

you put your head under.

Mulata in a Sarong

Light in her kitchen dilutes life to watercolor, frangipani
vined on the walls and in her curls. Honeybees now and then sip
at their centers. Buzz in her ears, studded with pearls.

Toasted plane of soft belly punctuated with a winking navel. Sarong
is emerald green, loosely tucked at rise of hipbone cupping copper light.
Beads hang between her breasts, jade and shaped like doves.

Her hair is loose and black, save for a shark bone comb with 3 long teeth
lodged at the nape of her neck. The tendrils could pinch a chopstick
on their own. They creep, like morning glories, to just beyond the rib.

She rakes her mane with her fingers. One might not be surprised
if music should pour from such strumming. Slender fingers
tug deftly through tangles. There is only one room.

The table, where you sit on a wobbly chair, is in the center. The bed,
in the corner. The sheets and tablecloth, cotton and clean but faded
and worn. Misted with rosewater. Back turned, she makes you tea.

A scar scaled with hexagons snakes down her spine.

She pours steeped roots & 3 peppercorns into your cup. It is hot and cracked
but mended. She whistles across it three times before handing it to you
with a raised eyebrow. A chipped plate of toast and marmalade.

You sip slowly. Look down at her bare feet with hard heels. Toes
painted cayenne. The ankles cross, knees parted like lips. A breeze
like breath lifts the sarong's hem. Makes way for the plea.

She sucks her teeth, sighs and asks. Once.
Only then do you look her in the eye. Do you say,
Yes. No matter the question.

Pangea

Aquila hands me a Ziploc bag
filled with pineapple rings thick and gold
as her Trini accent. They swim in cilantro,
black pepper, lime juice, flecks of red onion.

Her mouth, a conch shell blowing: *Chile, I come*
from a good colonial marriage—Mom's onliest
but I got more siblins than seeds in a papaya.

Caribbean islands each dem, afloat in one sea.
Neighbored, no bridge. How, on a map, it's clear

Africa   South America   puzzle pieces

on the table at finger's length.   Fish market girl,
gap in her teeth like mine.   Class bully,
held his pen funny   indented callous same as mine,
below the first knuckle.   Right middle finger.

His crooked signature matched my Daddy's. *Men be wave,*

women be shore. How it's always been. Since mem'ry
on this side, anyhow. Flip your eyes inside out,

they'll stay that way. Aquila's pineapple is bitter.

She puts vinegar in her mojo. *Spoils the sweet a bit,*
but ain't that life anyhow, dahlin? Build a bridge,

and get over it.

After Dinner

What is said in conversation
when all of the women leave
the room? Satin glove slipped
from fist. An uncut deck of cards.

The men show their teeth. Mark
opinions like territory. Laugh
upside down, wrinkles shape-
shifting between stone, wood

and flesh. This cut & paste debate
sits in the shade of cigar smoke.
Sips dark liquors neat, no chaser.
Spans home front and auction block.

Laughter and shit talk roll
like distant thunder. Make bridges
of fragments. End in guarded
embraces as quick as they are firm.

Never Saw it Coming

No faint whistle in the distance,
no set of flashing lights. You slipped

under my skin—a pulse,
open palm on stretched hide
the upbeat of my down time.

Hand on head on chest. Stroke of lock from root to tip,
along the shaft, between index & forefinger.
Rolling   back,   forth.

Inhale of breath between teeth—
a white skirt pulled up to the waist,
a flag on a balcony, released to the wind.

The last face I see before take off,
first upon landing. You carry my bag up
down the stairs, though I overpack.

Worry written on both sides
of heavy paper in your hand & mine.
Blue ink kissed by blue flame. Burned fingertip.

Ashes in a silver bowl.

Who knew I was such a tiny orange, so
easily peeled with one hand? Pistachio
lips parted for the cracking.

Mariu

We dance barefoot
Remedios Varo to the East, Jimi
Hendrix to the West.

Drinking white wine tinged with green, we crack
a hairline in your glass with our *Salud!* Eye to eye
and hit the table.

Listen:
Broccoli spores and burnt garlic that cling to ears of orrechiete, pressed
to the bowl. You made a bowl out of a carrot. And an apple.
And a cassis soda can. Mae West

backed by Duke Ellington on vinyl. In clean
dishtowels, we wring out defrosted spinach, toss with raisins,
parmesan and pine nuts. Line a glass pie pan
with stretched dough, slicing veins into tiny leaves
cut out of the extra. *Y ahora, las verenjenas...*

That day before New Year's Eve, when we bought
Panetonne, a case of Prosecco and stopped by the botanica
Cubana *porque ese chico presumido no sabia quien eres.*

The bunches of sage we dried upside down to burn in his footsteps.
Flowers for tea to wash your hair. Your ex who said no problem, came over,
blew cigar smoke, spit rum and feathers. Spent the night.

Cheap cheese and expensive chocolate with sea salt.
The cutting board. Alici anchovies dressed in lemon and
white lace. A tiny ceramic bowl for olive pits.

I have never met your mother but pledge allegiance
to her tiramisu. Sun salutations

on a roof in India at dawn. The sleeping courtyard,
the garlands of laundry like prayer flags, taunting the darkness
as if it were a bull. Mariu, who loves tiny things. Charms
and trinkets that fit in the palm of a fist, closed
and raised to the sky.

Amber

"Denying her wounds came from the same source as her power."
- Adrienne Rich

I'm brown, like the husk of a coconut
or a well seasoned calabash. Cracked more than once
but stronger for the mending. Fill me.
I won't leak a drop. Brown

as ancient tree resin. Prehistoric spiders
and secrets trapped in my drippings. Hardened,
preserved, moment suspended. Untouched
by continental shift or time. Brown

with full lips and white teeth that slice
a crescent moon into my face when I smile.
A gap in my teeth I once heard is prized
somewhere in Africa—means you got a "sweet pot." Brown

and over being cast as not enough, supporting role,
or an acquired taste. No pointed nose to sniff in apology.
No obedient wave to my nappy hair, coiled like DNA,
helix twists of whip & tongue lash. Brown,

tall and I don't slouch. Looking down on or up at,
but always in the eye. Grown enough to say, *fuck it.*
Danced with enough devils at enough crossroads,
to know life goes on. So why bother? Brown

as the dust I leave in my wake. As the paper bag
your mama packed a lunch in so you could pass
the test, or travel safe on a full stomach. Brown
as good furniture passed from one generation to the next,

kept in the family. Polished. A chest to hold your memories,
a bookcase to store your knowledge. A table, to balance
your plate on its head. A rocking chair, to soothe

and support your tired ass.

Notes

1. "Lime Pickle" is an ekphrastic poem inspired by artist Kathy Sosa's painting "Olivia's Offerings."

2. "Uplift the Race" refers to the historic Black American philosophy of racial uplift. "Amidst the violent racism prevalent at the turn of the twentieth century, African American cultural elites, struggling to articulate a positive black identity, developed a middle-class ideology of racial uplift. Insisting that they were truly representative of the race's potential, black elites espoused an ethos of self-help and service to the black masses and distinguished themselves from the black majority as agents of civilization; hence the phrase 'uplifting the race.' "(Uplifting the Race: Black Leadership, Politics & Culture in the Twentieth Century, Kevin K. Gaines, The University of North Carolina Press, 1996)

3. "Idlewild" and "Inkwell" refer to beach vacation resorts in Michigan and Martha's Vineyard, Massachusetts that were, and to some extent still are, thriving summer destinations for upper class Black Americans during segregation.

4. "Laius" refers to the Greek myth of a king of Thebes who attempted to slay the infant heir an oracle predicted was destined to kill him.

5. The phrase "day mark" refers to the distinguishing shape and color displayed on lighthouses to make them easily identifiable in daylight against background conditions.

6. "Mojo" refers to a typical Caribbean sauce/marinade made of garlic, olive oil and citrus juice.

about the author

**Lisa Pegram** is a DC native poet, essayist and lyricist. She has been published widely, including by the Academy of American Poets, Random House, Black Classic Press, The Independent film magazine, and L'Officiel, India. Her awards and honors include: a DC Artist Fellowship; Larry Neal Writer's Award Finalist; Uplifting Human Values Award; Art of Living Foundation; and the DC Mayor's Arts Award, "Outstanding Emerging Artist."

Pegram completed her MFA in Creative Writing at Lesley University in 2012 and is currently based in Curacao, Dutch Caribbean where she is a personal chef, freelance writer and professor at two universities.

Author photo credit: Kimberly C. Gaines